Highlights

Annelise Sievert

Highlights

By: *Annelise Sievert*

Around the World Publishing LLC
4914 Cooper Road Suite 144
Cincinnati, Ohio 45242-9998

    These stories are true. They are the memories that I carried with me for my life.
    Told to and written by Ron Mueller.

Highlights by Annelise Sievert**,** Copyright © 2011
Edited and republished by Ron Mueller, son. Copyright © 2022

    All rights reserved, including the right of reproduction, in whole or in part in any form.

ISBN 13: 978-1-68223-140-1
ISBN 10: 1-68223-140-2

Distributed by Ingram
Cover Picture by: Annelise Sievert
Cover Design by: Ron Mueller

Annelise Sievert

Highlights

Table of Content

Introduction 2021 by REM	1
Why do I write?	3
Do Blondes have more fun?	7
The Eucalyptus Tree	15
Christmas in the Tropics or Who got the first bite?	19
The Brazilian American	23
The Train, Are My Days Numbered?	27
Second Beginning	35
A Beautiful Shared Sunset	39
A Very Brave Lady by MH	43
Dancing	57
Always in my thoughts and Heart by CZM	63
Epilogue by REM	67
More About Annelise Sievert	71

Annelise Sievert

Highlights

Introduction
Forever More

The Irish Ridge,
    The mighty Little Flint.
        The squirrel in the lane.
            And then there was the train.
From Sao Paulo to New York
    The Inter Coastal Water way
        And Uwe in his quiet way
The road trip west
    That was the best
        As Kimmy put you to the test.
It's time once more to climb up high,
    Up to the top of your Eucalyptus friend
        So high you saw the world
            And felt the wind of life upon your face
            And saw the dreams of days to come.
    Nine lives indeed,
        Hit by a train,
            Hit on the brain
                You always walked away.
        You drove with friends
            You went from sea to sea
                You went from North to South
        You lived your life at God's given speed.
           You had nine lives and more.
And now goodbye
    Good journey,
        With love forever more.
            My goodbye to Mom
            June 2017

    And that was her last year. She made it to Ninety-one and a half.

    Highlights captures a few of her writings and stories.

Annelise Sievert

Highlights

Why do I write?
2011

The desire to write started many years back. I can't exactly remember when. The first time I thought of becoming a writer, was when I really started to enjoy reading books. I was then about fourteen and every moment I could find I went to a place where no one could disturb me and my reading.

My favorite place was an old Eucalyptus tree that none of the neighborhood children could climb up.

My mother could never find me to help her around the house. There high in the tree I would sit and read till dusk. I was a regular book worm and since I was of two nationalities, I read in two languages: Portuguese and German.

Mystery books were my favorite. Expedition stories, no matter where, captivated me. I lived and acted through many of the main character personalities.

Annelise Sievert

The story telling began when my two girlfriends left me alone for one summer. My brother, Conrad, five years younger than I, and his friend Peter, would wait for me to come home from school. I was the babysitter for my brother when Mother would go shopping. I had promised mother not to take my brother on any of "my dangerous expeditions."

This left me with little to do with him.

Then one rainy summer afternoon we were near an old cave left over from some past the revolution between the states of Sao Paulo and Minas Gerais. This was a secret cave I shared with my girlfriends June and Beling. I guided the two boys into the cave and my brother, and his friend became the focused on my telling of the story.

They loved it. After that we would often go to the cave where I would continue telling the latest story that I had thought up.

They accepted me because, I was a tomboy and able to out climb all the boys and girls in the neighborhood.

My story telling flowed from my imagination and the reading I had done or was doing. I adapted the stories for their age.

That summer was the start of my story telling. It went on for many years. It was at that time I began to imagine myself as a famous writer.

It was up there in the tree where my first idea of writing books as good as the writers I read started. I had a few stories in my mind and began putting them down on paper. I had many story ideas and I put them down in my "book."

Highlights

One day my father found my "book." He read it and laughed and made fun of it. That was the end for my writing. I would continue to think of stories, but I never took the chance of writing it down again.

Many years have passed since I first started to think about writing. Many things have happened to me during those years. Life's many turns seem to have intervened each time I made the attempt to write.

I married, had three children, divorced, immigrated to the United States, made my living as an insurance salesperson, taught ball room dancing, remarried twice, took up oil painting and tried several times at sharpening my writing skills. I attended writing school and my dream seemed much closer. But I also realized it was much more difficult than I had imagined. I found out, writing is a real art and the thoughts one might have sound so different once put on paper.

It never dawned on me that one day when I was old, I would sit down and put it all to paper. Now at eighty-five, grandmother of eight, great grandmother of eleven, I am once again "putting pen to paper."

The saying is, *"It's never too late."*

Well, I hope this is true.

So, let's try it one more time.

This time I have enrolled the help of my son, Ron who also aspires to write.

Annelise Sievert

Highlights

Do Blondes have more fun?

"No!" would have been my answer many years ago.

My story begins when my parents, who originally tried to emigrate from Germany in 1924 to the United States, were denied a visa and ended up in Brazil instead.

I look back and call it fate.

On their trip to Brazil by ship they met some Catholic Priests who knew Brazil.

My Father, a Mechanical Engineer, learned of a job in Itajuba a small town in the state of Minas Gerais almost in the middle of Brazil. Once there he became a teacher in a small college. He became well known in the town. He continued to follow his ambition and a few years later he managed to open his own business.

Annelise Sievert

A year after we arrived in Itajuba, I was born. I became the most famous towhead around the neighborhood.

At first mother could not figure out why everyone paid so much attention to me. Strangers would come to visit and would ask to see the baby. Soon however she discovered the reason was my blond hair and blue eyes and very fair complexion.

Most of the people were either Indian mixed with Portuguese or Black or a mix of everything.

We were the only foreign white family in the region.

My parents hardly spoke any Portuguese and did not understand the conversations about my complexion and my mother could not tell them not to make such a fuss over me.

Things got out of hand one day when I was about two. Mother was taking me for a walk. A lady who met us on the street talked to mother for a second and then picked me up and calling to some neighbors disappeared with me into one of the houses.

Imagine the panic my mother felt at having her baby carried away. She rushed after the lady and when my mother finally caught up all the women were admiring me with, "Oh's! And Ahs! And what eyes, what skin and oh the hair!"

Mother was too frightened to say anything. Finally, when she could, she picked me up and without saying anything she walked out of the place.

From then on, she kept me in the backyard where I would play with my sister, who was older and had dark hair. For years I thought my sister was so lucky to be dark haired.

Highlights

Then when I was four, I went to kindergarten. My teacher was a family friend and she called me her angel. French Nuns ran the school. They thought of me as their angel.

Soon I was to be the "Angel" for every special occasion. I was the angel for all the Church festivities where an angel would look good. My angel outfits, one in every pastel color with a variety of silver and gold stars were long and the wings were made of real feathers. I would wear a silver or golden band on my head to match the color of the stars on my dress.

Many times, my mother would get disgusted about constantly having to take me here or there or to walk in processions. But the Sisters had a way of making her understand and I kept being the "Angel."

It is always surprising to me that angels were thought of as blond and blue eyed when all the figures in the bible were dark haired and had brown eyes.

Then came the terrible day when the sisters discovered that their blond "Angel" could also be a Devil. I was always doing something that could have gotten me into trouble, but most things were just overlooked.

There were several instances I remember but the funniest I think was when I was standing up in the choir loft, looking down as the nuns where coming, two by two, down the center aisle, into the chapel. Something inside me kept telling me how nice it would be to spit on one of the Sisters head.

"Bet you can't hit one of on top of their head," a little voice inside my head kept saying.

So, I leaned forward, aimed and I spit. Wham, it was a direct hit. Immediately, I knew I should not have done it. I tried to believe it had not been me. I was spotted immediately, and I can still see the disappointed faces of the Nuns who later scolded me.

But there is more. Another time I hid myself in senile, Sister Anne's room. I didn't understand her condition. The only thing I knew was she would do anything I asked her to do. One day I wanted to stay at the convent, but I knew my mother wouldn't let me. So, I talked Sister Anne into dressing me in one of her habits. As the time came for me to go home no one could find me. I was in the Chapel kneeling down for at least an hour. Then when I thought the Sisters had given up I began to leave but all the Sisters were coming for their afternoon prayer. So, I knelt down, bent my head, and pretended to be in deep prayer. I was not found out until supper time.

Again, I was scolded but this time the Nuns had to hide their smiles. Pictures were taken of the "Little Nun." My departure from the convent was very different from my reception that I received when I arrived home.

After a few questions, I was given a good spanking by my father and was put to bed.

Things changed in the little town of Itajuba over the nine years my family lived there.

Highlights

World War two was on the horizon. There was a lot of anti-German propaganda broadcast throughout Brazil.

Going to school began to be a hateful experience. Kids would tease me and make rhymes with "blond hair, blue eyed people" and words which weren't kind or nice to be said.

Father, who by this time ran his own business, also noticed a different attitude of the people. When I came home one day crying because the boys had teased me and even thrown stones at me, I heard Father tell Mother that as soon as school was over, we would all be moving to Sao Paulo.

So, the family moved to the big industrial city of Sao Paulo. It was big at that time and now days it is one of the biggest industrial cities in the world. There were lots of foreigners and what luck, lots of blonds too. Once again, I was normal. For a few years I forgot the episode of being blonde and being different in coloring.

I was a teenager when one day my girlfriend and I were walking downtown, and some man passed us and said something.

My girlfriend turned to me and said, "It's all because of your blond hair. Mine use to be like yours but thank God, it darkened before I was twelve and you would never have known I was blond."

I looked surprised at her not quite grasping what she meant.

"Well," she went on, "The only blond girls, grown up ones, I mean, are the bleached blond and not so nice and kind, who work the streets."

That evening I went home and informed my mother I wanted to tint my hair black. Of course, I didn't get the permission.

Annelise Sievert

World War two started in Europe and things became very difficult in Brazil for those of German heritage. Talk of entering the war and soldiers being drafted was discussed. The German families, even those who had been in Brazil for several generations had their homes searched for guns, radio transmitters and other things considered contraband. Anything confiscated was never returned, even after the war.

I had graduated from High School and had been accepted to a nursing school in Rio de Janeiro. It was during this period that the University Students rioted. They created general mayhem by breaking the windows of suspected businesses and of homes of those they believed were on the German side.

The ignorance and general animosity were tremendous.

Any foreign language was taken as German. Many times, Americans or Englishmen were beaten, and things taken from them.

Even the police could not solve this problem.

I was frightened to walk on the streets. I had read in the Newspaper what they were doing to girls, especially blond ones. They would carry them through the streets playing "ping, pong" and doing other humiliating things to them.

One day, after a three-hour practice at the hospital, I took the streetcar to my normal drop off on my way home. After the drop off, I had a long walk to where I lived.

Highlights

Suddenly, I noticed a commotion at the end of the street. I stopped to look at what was going on and froze. I wanted to run but my legs just wouldn't move.

Around twenty students were singing and laughing and making speeches. They seemed like a crazy bunch. What really frightened me was the blond girl they had in their arms. She was crying and trying to get loose, but they were carrying her. They were laughing and carrying on.

They spotted me. I was unable to run. They surrounded me. I don't know what they were saying. One fellow said something, and they turned around and went on down the street.

Then it hit me. My nurse's uniform had saved me from the ill fate of the other girl.

I remember the last words he said, "She must be an American. Look at her nurses' uniform."

So, my experiences extended from being and "Angel" to being totally scared of being blonde.

Though I thought multiple times about it, I never tinted my hair any other color. My hair darkened a little naturally but always remained blonde.

A few years later, I married and had three children: one girl and two boys. The boys were as blond and towheaded as I had been. My daughter had ash blond hair that darkened. I was so happy for her.

Many years later when she was a teenager, she told me how much she would have loved being as blond as I had been. How could I tell her, or have her understand how things were for me when I was her age? How could I tell her how much I had wanted her hair color?

All I could do was to smile.

Highlights

The Eucalyptus Tree

I can still close my eyes and see myself walking down the broad red dirt street and standing in front of the house I grew up in during my teenage years. I see trees all around. Most of the trees are Eucalyptus trees.

Sao Paulo was known for its Eucalyptus trees. We had only one neighbor near our home. All around was the forest. This was the area known as "Alte da boa Vista" – "Heights of the good view. It was a ten-minute walk up hill from the streetcar and a forty-five minute ride to Sao Paulo. All we could see from our house was trees and wilderness. I thought of the view as having a vision of paradise.

There was one giant Eucalyptus just outside of the wall to our yard.

I was twelve when we moved in. I had two good friends. During school breaks, we would meet under this tree to decide what to do for the day. Together we climbed many trees, rode horseback, went swimming, bicycling and went hiking. We were the neighborhood "tom girls."

Every day we would try to climb our "Eucalyptus" friend outside the gate. It was one of the largest trees around. Its first branch was about ten feet from the ground. We would try to toss a rope over the first branch, but we always failed.

There was one boy in the neighborhood that could climb up the tree, but I made the observation that he only dared to go halfway up the tree.

Then during my second summer, my girlfriends both went to England on vacation. I was left alone. I was now thirteen, maybe five foot two and had grown about as tall as I would ever get. I went to the tree and was lost sitting watching hundreds of bees swarming and sipping the nectar of the white Eucalyptus flower clusters.

Suddenly, more determined than ever, I began throwing the rope up towards the first branch. After several attempts, I was lucky. The rope went up and over the first branch.

I was able to pull and climb up to the first branch. There I had to stop and recover. I was shaky and all scratched up from the rough bark. I was breathless but so very happy.

Highlights

The climb to the very top was much easier. I don't know how to put into words the exhilaration and overwhelming feeling that went through me as I reached the very top limbs. I was clinging to the thin top branches and the wind was swinging me back and forth.

I could see for miles around.

I wasn't lonely any more I had conquered my old friend the tree and it had rewarded me with letting me see all the natural beauty stretching out for miles around.

That night I was the happiest thirteen-year-old girl in the world. I had a friend no one else had, and it was all mine.

I have never forgotten that friend who shared all my dreams for many more years. Even now when the Eucalyptus flowers bloom, I close my eyes and I return back to that house, that tree and I remember the hours I spent sitting up in its branches reading and dreaming what the future would bring.

Many things that happened in the future were to be both pleasant and unpleasant experiences. The fact that the future is unknown is life's way of keeping us engaged.

Annelise Sievert

Highlights

Christmas in the Tropics or Who got the last bite?

Christmas in the tropics is never white Christmas. Germany has always been famous for how it celebrates and glorifies the Christmas celebration. Mother grew up in a family that always made Christmas a special event.

Even after several years of having lived in Brazil, Mother had not adjusted too well. Christmas was always the time of year when the differences in weather and customs became really obvious. Mother's emotional ties with Christmas surfaced and distressed her. She would always mention that she missed the snow and the other festivities of Christmas that was commonplace in Germany.

Church of course had the festivity, and I would play the angel because of my blue eyes and blond hair. But there were no real Christmas trees like she enjoyed in Germany. There were no chocolate ornaments to hang on the tree. There were no special sweet bakery goods to serve.

Each year we would hear her sigh, "If there were just snow," for almost every day before Christmas.

Then one year my father's sister came to visit. She brought some chocolate Christmas ornaments.

Diamonds would not have had the result the two boxes of chocolate ornaments had on my mother. She was transported back to her younger years. She decided to stage Christmas the way it was done in Germany.

Soon the living room was off limits to my sister and me.

Father had gotten a tree out of the woods. It was the best he could do to match the look my mother was expecting.

My older sister understood my mother better than I. I had never seen snow or experienced any Christmas other than the ones in Brazil. All I knew was Christmas was my favorite time of year and my January one birthday followed soon after.

My only complaint was that often my Christmas gifts were also my birthday gifts. I may have gotten extra but I was never sure about that.

Not to be able to go into the living room and waiting nervously to hear the little silver bells announcing Santa's arrival was all I could handle. The day finally arrived where we would be able to go into the living room.

It was hard to remember the verse we had to learn and that we were expected to say in front of Santa.

I was a bundle of thrill and expectation.

Highlights

Finally, the bells announcing that it was time made a faint ringing noise.

The living room door was opened. The room was dark.

The candles were lit on the tree. Everything was so beautiful.

We were told to say our verse for Santa who we could not see, but we were sure that he was standing in the back of the room.

The ornaments were glittering, and the chocolate smell permeated the air and made such a wonderful smell.

We went through the expected formalities.

Father finally put the lights on.

The lights came on and my mother let out a loud, "No." and burst into tears.

We all tried to understand why she was crying, what was bothering her so terribly.

Then we all saw the ten-inch-wide swath of ants going up the tree. They were eating our chocolate ornaments.

Some ornaments were also dripping because of the heat of the candles and the general heat of the room.

Father reacted swiftly. He took the fire bucket and soaked the tree, the ornaments, and the ants.

By this time, I was crying too.

My sister helped in getting more water while I and mother consoled each other. I was crying about the loss of chocolate.

But my mother like all good mothers had saved some ornaments for later. She had planned to let us eat the ornaments on the tree and then surprise us later with a few more.

So, the ants got the first bite of our Christmas chocolate, but we got ours as well. We got the last bite!

There were no other Christmas's that lived up to the one where Chocolate ornaments were involve. After that, the ornaments were beautiful glass ones that Mother began to collect.

Highlights

The Brazilian American

My parents originally tried to emigrate from Germany in 1924 to the United States. They were denied a visa. My father had already purchased his tickets on a ship to the United States. However, when he went to the American Embassy, to get a visa, they explained to him that the quota for Germans was closed for that year.

The rampant inflation in Germany at the time made getting a refund on the tickets almost worthless. Disgusted he went to restaurant near the embassy. He was sipping a beer in deep thought trying to overcome his deep disappointment and to figure out what to do next. America had been his dream destination. Waiting for another year seemed impossible for him and his wife and a three-year-old daughter. The rampant inflation would make him penniless in that time.

A young man sitting at the next table addressed my father, "You seem perturbed about something. "I can I be of help?"

"Yes, I am," said my father and proceeded to tell of his plight.

The man replied, "We don't have quotas in Brazil, why don't you exchange your tickets? The same ship company goes to Brazil. You will be welcome there."

So as fate would have it, my father took his family and moved to Brazil. On their trip to Brazil by ship they met some Catholic Priests who spoke German and knew Brazil. Father, who was a Mechanical Engineer, learned of an opportunity as a professor of Math in Itajuba a small town in the state of Minas Gerais almost in the middle of Brazil. There he became a teacher in a small college.

"Numbers are the only common language all over the world," he used to say.

After a few years as a professor, he managed to open his own business.

We lived in Itajuba until I was nine or ten. Then we moved to Sao Paulo. There I went to High School and later with the grudging acceptance of my father I went to nurses training in Rio de Janeiro.

I met a handsome young man named Edgar Muller. I had three children. However, Edgar had a wandering eye and was out with other women. That was the end of my romance with Edgar.

Brazil was a very strict Catholic country with no divorce laws. The only recourse would be to get a divorce through the Church. Such a thing almost always took years to get processed.

Meanwhile the Müller side of the family wanted to put my kids in a private care facility where each side of the family could visit. This was quite upscale and fancy, but it was not for my children.

Highlights

With the help of my Father and the American friends, Ross, and Georgia Kitzmiller, who sponsored me, I was able to get visas to come to the United States. In January 1955, I landed in Miami and then went on to Chicago. The Kitzmiller's met us there and took us into their home until I could get on my own two feet. Ross helped me get a job at the Air Force PX in Rantoul, Illinois.

In those days there was no family support. As a woman, the pay at the PX where I worked was half of what the men made. When I objected, the manager pointed out the men had families to support. Sounds logical, unless you were a single mother with three kids and there was no welfare support in those days. In search of a way to make a better income, I became an insurance salesperson. It was hard to convince some people that a woman could sell insurance, but my drive and need made me one of the top sales representatives.

From the beginning I fell in love with this country. I was able to make my opportunities happen. As soon as I could, I officially became a US citizen and made sure my children did too.

Today I will say I am American.

When my Father died, I returned to Brazil and lived there briefly. My father had willed me a rather large piece of land and I hoped to do something for my family with it. As it turned out, Father had been swindled and the deed to the land was not truly his. I ended up with nothing.

I returned to the US to get re-established, Marlene and Conrad stayed in Brazil. On my return, I felt I was home. My parents never understood my love for the US, but I have experienced the opportunity it provides.

Then it was time to return and bring them back as well.

I bought passage on the ship Burg Sparenburg where I met Hans Uwe Sievert. This was my true love. Things happen for a reason. Meeting him on my trip to Brazil was my reward sent by my father. He must have felt bad as he looked down from heaven.

I have seen it grow.

My children have done well, and it appears my Grandchildren are also doing well.

God Bless America.

Highlights

The Train, Are My Days Numbered?

I was following a gas truck that was going fast on the Iowa country gravel road. The gravel was falling from the truck and dust was flying up and out from the back wheels. I was following the truck and having had a hard time. I was trying to decide between falling back or trying to pass.

The December morning was dry, and winter was in the air.

I was enjoying my new Ford station wagon. This was a new 1960 model, and it was a beauty. The heater was going and so was the radio. I had just bought the car three months ago when I moved from Illinois to Iowa. It was not the sports car I had dreamed of, but it was new and had the latest features.

Dirt and gravel were being thrown out to the sides by the truck. To avoid all the flying gravel, I moved in close behind the truck. The truck had stickers on the bumper, and I was able to read them.

Then I spotted something moving off to the right. What was it? Nervously I looked back to the truck. There were no brake lights. The sticker I was reading so avidly only a moment earlier said, "We stop at all railroad crossings." Instead, the truck picked up speed and went speeding away.

Something was not right. There… a gray giant was charging toward me from the right. If a whistle had been blowing, I did not hear it because of the closed window and the radio and heater noise. There it was a gigantic and powerful freight train bearing down on my car.

The brakes did not help. I put it into second gear. Instant panic and then finally resignation as the car skidded in toward the tracks.

I knew I was history. I instinctively turned off the ignition key and closed my eyes.

Then, crunch, crunch, crunch.

I clutched the steering wheel with both hands. The car shuddered and shook but did not move. I was afraid to open my eyes. I knew by the sounds that my car must be in bad shape. I seemed to be alright. Finally, I opened my eyes.

My purse had fallen and dumped its contents on the floor. I bent down and gathered everything up and put it back into my purse. I tried to open the driver's door, but it would not open. I scooted across the seat and tried the passenger door.

It opened and I climbed out of the car. I stood and looked at the front of my car and then towards the train.

Highlights

The train had stopped, and three or four men were running toward me.

"There she is. Thank God she's alive and getting out of the car," I heard one of the men say.

I felt as if I was in a dream. Most of what was said did not register. I was absently checking the contents of my purse to see if my new lipstick was in it.

"Are you OK? Do you need help?" one of the men asked.

"No, I'm Ok," I heard someone say and then realized I was the one answering. I really was not OK. I was confused. I had no clue what I should do but I was very independent and disliked taking help.

The men started back toward the train. They were saying it was a miracle the car was not dragged down the tracks and that the driver had lived through it. One of the men turned back and asked if they should call the authorities or someone else.

"Thank you, No, I am going to that farmhouse," I said pointing to a yellow house and barn. Neither I nor the man noticed that it was old and abandoned.

The men went on down the track. When back on the train, one of the men called the dispatcher to let him know about the accident and the location. The dispatcher notified the authorities.

I looked at my car and realized the entire front end had been cut off. The front bumper, radiator and head lights were gone. The three-month-old station wagon had lost its shine. I was not sure how I would get the car moved. I hoped no other trains were scheduled to come by any time soon.

With these thoughts I walked toward the farmhouse. Then I realized it looked abandoned. I had no other choice but to walk on to the next farmhouse. The walk was hot and tiring. At the second farmhouse gate I called to the people I hoped would be in the house. No one came out. I was looking around for other farmhouses when the TV repair man came out onto the porch.

"Who are you looking for ma'am," he inquired.

I explained my situation and ordeal.

"May I please use the phone?" I asked.

"I'm sorry; I can't let you in to use the phone. It would be against company policy," the TV repairman said. He was not sure what was going on.

I felt insulted. "Look out there at the railroad crossing. That is what is left of my car after being hit by a train." I said pointing to my car visible even at this distance across the flat Iowa plain.

"Wow, I didn't see it happen. I had the TV apart on the floor," the repairman replied.

"Come on in but make sure they are only local calls," the repairman said as he led the way to the phone.

I called the police, the car insurance representative and finally I called a friend to come and get me up.

Highlights

The police were first to arrive. I rode with the sheriff back to the car. The sheriff and his deputy walked around her car. They were talking quietly and pointing down the track at the various pieces of the car.

"You are really a lucky lady. Never saw a car, train wreck that ended up so clean," was the sheriff's comment.

"Tell me what happened, but before you do, please let me have your license," the Sheriff asked.

I told him about the gravel truck and trying to avoid the spraying gravel and the last-minute realizing that the train was bearing down on me. I noticed the sheriff did not seem to be paying attention.

"Oh my, your driver's license expired a year ago," the sheriff said as he put down his radio mike.

"No, No," I replied. My birthday is on January the first and this is December.

"I'm sorry, but you are one year overdue," the sheriff replied pointing at the license.

After a few moments the sheriff went on, "Look, I will just write out a warning for the overdue license. Let's focus on the train-car accident. Tell me again what happened so I can get it down on this form."

The sheriff's deputy was dragging the various pieces of the car back from where they had been dragged by the train.

"I'll call for a wrecker to come and take your car to the County lot. We'll hold it there until you get your license and arrange for the car to get fixed.

Nelly, my friend arrived.

"My golly, what in the world happened?" she said looking at the front of the car and all the pieces the deputy had piled up.

"Who are you?" the sheriff inquired.

"I'm Annelise's friend. She called and said she needed a ride home," Nelly said.

"Well Nelly, it seems your friend took on the Burlington Railroad and lived to talk about it," the sheriff said with a smile. "Why don't you get her home? I think she has had enough excitement for one day."

I gave Nelly a hug. I was not sure about how I was going to tell my husband about the car. I had to tell the entire story to Nelly.

"You always do the wildest things and get away with them. Now you live to talk about a train wreck. Nothing exciting ever happens to me," Nelly said as she drove across the bridge leading to my house.

Three days later, I began crying incoherently as I watched my three children walking up the driveway. I was thinking about the day I had met their school bus by the bridge to give them a ride home. The driveway is at least a mile long. On the way back, a squirrel had run out in front of the car, and I had instinctively swerved to miss it. The car had ended up in the ditch. The three had all walked home the rest of the way.

I thought back at other near misses. I counted more than a handful. Nine lives; cats have nine lives, but I am no cat. Was this a warning? Were my days numbered and what number was I on?

Highlights

Nine lives indeed. A million miles have gone by, and I have survived them all. Miles of ice and snow, of sun and heat, I always made my way.

I drove alone.

I drove with friends.

I drove the across the desert and up the mountains then down to the sea.

I drove from North to South and East to West.

I drove across the land.

My days are numbered.

My hair is now grey the highlight of long living.

I have had nine lives and more.

They were all interesting and wonderful lives.

Annelise Sievert

Highlights

Second Beginning

My father had died. He had put me in his will. My mother had come to the US. She returned and escorted my daughter and son. I stayed behind to complete my tuberculosis treatment.

My middle child, as stubborn as I had been when I was growing up was determined to finish his senior year in High School at Burlington High. He was hosted by the Persky family and would be able to fulfill his wish.

Little did he know what the road ahead had in store for him.

This was an emotional time for me.

I felt a responsibility to go home and see if I could turn the inheritance of a large plot of land to the advantage of my immediate family. I really would have preferred to keep my family together in the U.S.

Finally, it was time for me to go to Brazil. I booked a freighter out of New York. It was inexpensive and I figured it would give me time to continue my recovery.

This was my first time in New York. I had arrived by train to New York from Burlington Iowa. I could not afford a grand hotel, so I stayed at the YWCA overnight.

I took a taxi to go to the ship I was traveling to Brazil on. I was to board the Burg Sparenburg, a freighter that took a limited number of passengers. I was an hour late.

How could I have known there was more than one Pier Two? The taxi driver, with a New York lack of sensitivity, told me I would never make it in time to Pier Two in the Aery Basin in Brooklyn.

I was upset but told him to try.

I even thought maybe he had kidnapped me because of the neighborhood we were driving through. Finally, the driver announced we were at the gate leading to the piers. I was about to get out when the gate guard checked my passport and told the taxi driver to take me right to the ship. My taxi drove right up to the gang way of the German freighter.

The Chief Stewart, in very broken English, tried to explain to me, that they had been trying to contact me. They would have left me if I had not just arrived when I did. Suddenly, I was not sure I really wanted to go. My reception was somewhat cool, though I understood the fact they were trying to stay on schedule.

Highlights

I could have told him my whole story about never having been in New York before, about giving the wrong address to the taxi driver.

I could have done this in German. I am sure he would have appreciated this, but I just said a few words in English excusing the delay. I was greeted by the First Officer who was also telling me he was ready to give the orders to pull the gangway up.

As soon as I climbed the gang way and my luggage was brought up, the gangway was raised.

I was glad to have my cabin shown to me. I closed the door to the room. I could feel the pressure fall as I sat on the edge of the bed. I freshened up and felt relieved to be on board. My reception was not as warm as I had expected. I wasn't really angry. I couldn't blame the ships officers my since I was the one an hour and a half late.

I felt the ship moving. I finally dared to slip out of my room. I wanted to take some pictures of New York City. I had only arrived the day before and this was really my first opportunity to see the city. The other twelve passengers and some of the officers were on deck.

We left the ugly old part of Brooklyn's Pier 2.

The Statue of Liberty was back lighted by the last rays of the setting Sun.

I was fascinated by Manhattan's skyline.

Then this huge, beautiful bridge caught my attention. Next to me was a fellow taking pictures. He told me the bridge was the famous Verrazano Bridge, the largest suspension bridge in the world.

I looked at him not quite sure if he was a Boy Scout Master, a passenger on the ship or one of the ship's crew. His uniform didn't impress me. He had short pants and shoes that did not match his outfit. I asked him if he was a passenger.

"I am often told that sometimes it looks like I am," he replied with a smile. He introduced himself as Hans.

I thanked him and walked down along the ships rail toward the bow.

Later I learned he was the Chief engineer.

Life always gave me surprises.

Little did I know that six months later he would be my husband.

Highlights

A Beautiful Shared Sunset
February 2001

    Uwe's passing was a very sad moment for me. It was also a relief because he died of Lou Gehrig's disease that robbed him of speech and all motor abilities. He was bed ridden for almost two years.

    The family and many friends came for his funeral. He had spent thirty years at sea as a Chief Engineer on various merchant ships.

    I met him the first time on my way to back to Brazil when my brother purchased me a ticket home to Brazil. He thought the time would help me to rest after my bought with TB.

    Uwe was the love of my life.

    His ashes were spread in the Gulf of Mexico. I vowed to join him when it was my time.

    He loved the water and had wanted his ashes spread at sea. His wish came true. After the ashes were slowly eased into the waters and riding the waves, each person tossed a rose. One by one each member of the family and friends, threw them gently into the waves.

After the late afternoon ceremony, most of the family and friends sat on the beach and watched a lovely sunset.

The next few days everyone returned home. They had to get back to their lives and jobs.

The house seemed empty. I felt alone.

I was not alone. Kimmy had stayed.

She and Fred, our basset got along well, and she was down at the lake with him.

I was walking around the house thinking about all the good years Uwe and I had together. I went to the room where he had stayed for almost two years. I was not sure what I had to do. My eyes fell on the hospital bed. Then they went to the red colored hummingbird feeders outside of window. Uwe had loved his hummingbirds. They had been the single joy that he had until the end.

The little birds were feeding and fighting as they always did. Would they miss him? I'm sure they would miss their buddy of two years. When still able to be in his wheelchair he had sat out there daily and knew how many and at what time they would show.

"Oma"! Kimmy's voice came from a distant reminiscent world. I was crying silently.

Kimmy wiped my tears off as she said that I should come outside and play with Freddy and her.

I looked at my beautiful granddaughter who was thirteen going on twenty.

I joint the two and we walked along the lake.

Highlights

The next day one of my lakeside neighbors volunteered to house and dog sit and suggested that the two of us go on a road trip.

Both Kimmy and I thought it was a great Idea.

We accepted the offer and took off the next day.

We sat in the car, and I drove to Tallahassee.

I had no clue what we were going to do.

The first night we stayed in a hotel close to the Capitol. Together we studied the map.

We decided to go down towards the Gulf via Apalachicola. Then we would head back to Defuniak Springs.

After Kim went to sleep I studied the map some more and decided to first go to Wakulla Springs. I had heard of Wakulla but had never been there.

I thanked God double that night, for my children and their support, for Kimmie who had volunteered to stay with me. I was so thankful in my desolate stage, to have her there.

We were doing what we both liked. We were traveling!

The day in Wakulla was so breathtaking. The trip in the boat, the birds, the alligators, snakes, turtles, the swamp in general and our guide, he was a good storyteller. Most of it seemed true and some of it I am sure he made up. We didn't care we enjoyed the stories.

After lunch we continued down to Apalachicola around the bay towards Panama City. We stopped short of getting into the city and stayed in a very nice motel.

We were just in time to see the most gorgeous sunset on the Gulf.

Kimmy never had seen such a beautiful one and commented that they didn't have ones like it in Illinois!

We both sat on the beach watching the waves, which seemed to be playing with the sunrays which were stroking them lovingly.

The sunset was very similar to the one we had experienced off of Destin. It was a beautiful sunset. One that none of us will ever forget.

That evening nothing was said.

Next day on the drive home Kim said, " Oma, you and I were thinking the same thing last night, weren't we? "

I turned to her and gave her the best smile I could manage between my rolling tears and nodded my head.

Kimmie stayed another month then she had to go home to Illinois.

She and I formed a strong bond.

Little did I know that Kimmie and I would make a much grander trip a few years later.

Highlights

A Very Brave Lady
By Marlene Hart, her daughter

I have always thought of my mother as a very brave lady.

On January 20th, 1955, she left Brazil to seek a new life in America. She left with three young children. I was nine and a half. Ronald was seven and a half. Conrad who was only one and a half. We all rode to the airport from the fazenda or ranch in one of our uncle Kutty's delivery trunks.

The ride to the airport seemed to go on forever but the details at the airport escape me. We finally got on to the plane and I remember we sat in middle seats. We traveled overnight and in the early morning landed in Miami.

The shining sun, the balmy temperature caused our mother to leave us in our warm weather clothing.

Then a short time later we boarded our second plane and flew on to O'Hare Airport.

There we were met by Ross Kitzmiller, our sponsor. He had used his connections to arrange to meet our plane out on the tarmac.

It was very cold and large sparkling snowflakes engulfed us. We had never seen snow before. I remember Ron walking with his mouth open trying to eat the snow.

Luckily, Ross had brought heavy duty jackets for all of us. He hurried us into the car, and we left the Chicago airport. It was a long ride south to Rantoul.

Ross worked at the Rantoul Airforce Base and lived in a small but wonderfully comfortable house in Rantoul. Georgia and the enticing aroma of hot cocoa greeted us as we entered the house.

The Kitzmillers had been our backdoor neighbors in Brazil. They were our sponsors to the US.

Highlights

We lived with the Kitzmiller for a brief period of time. Two things stand out in my mind. We never sat down to a meal that one of the five kids at the table would spill their milk. Ross responded with a growl that would have scared a lion to let us know his displeasure. He always scared us. The second was that we had corn flakes for breakfast. This was something that I liked, and it was something I never had before.

We moved into a small trailer. Tiny is a better description. Today it would not make the grade of a good camper. There was one bunkbed for Ron and me. Con slept on a padded mat beside the bunkbed. Mom slept on the sofa. It was small but it was home and comfortable.

Mom was a very hard worker and always strived to do better. I remember her working at Chanute Air Force Base PX while we lived in Rantoul. She struggled to make ends meet. She got paid on Saturday and on Friday we were often looking at an empty refrigerator.

The Kitzmiller's knew of her struggles and often invited us for a Friday evening dinner. We always looked forward to one of Georgia's meals and survived every spilled glass of milk.

A year or so later, Mom learned she was making less than half of what the male clerks doing exactly what she did. She decided that she had to make a change so she could feed her children. She learned that she could sell insurance and keep the royalty she got for each sale.

We moved to Urbana, Illinois. She was incredibly good at selling insurance. She almost immediately had an income that allowed her to buy a larger trailer that had beds for all of us. There was a small kitchen and the pantry and refrigerator had food in it. The front door opened into the front sitting area.

A short time later she was able to move us into a house that had been converted to be two apartments. The house was only a few city blocks from the University of Illinois campus. Ron got the job of cleaning the clinkers out of the coal fired heater of the house and earned a few pennies.

While at the apartment a car hit Conrad as he chased a ball into the street. Georgia came over and met Ron. I came home from school and learned of the accident. It was scarry but he was only badly bruised and frightened.

Highlights

Mom began dating during this time. I remember meeting some of her dates, but none became serious.

Our duplex neighbor, our friend Evelyn had her brother Buck visiting. She had us over for dinner. He was ruggedly handsome. He and mom dated and a few months later they married. She became Annelise LaMar.

After they were married, we moved to Burlington, Iowa where Buck lived. They found a place in the country. It was a place that became a state park. It was an old farmhouse built into a hillside. The house, more than a hundred years old had first floor with narrow windows that had been built, to be barricaded, to fight the Indians. The back of the house was under ground and stayed at a constant forty-five degrees. This was the room that serve to hold all our canned goods and the potatoes stored in straw. It housed a large freezer that was always filled with a variety meat.

Out about a football field's length to the front of the house a small river, more like a large creek ran at the base of a cliff that rose more than a hundred feet as it reached for the sky.

The mile long lane crossed the Flint over an old bridge to the main wide gravel road. We would walked each morning out to the main road to catch the school bus. It took us out away from Burlington to a one room sandstone schoolhouse where Mrs. Henry taught grades one through eight.

Mom worked in the office of a major electronic assembly factory in West Burlington. Buck worked as a heavy-duty bucket operator for a construction company. During the school year we went to school and during the summer we were home on the farm. We had chores to do, but the creek and wandering the woods were the main activities.

The land was too rugged to farm but there was a large garden that mom and Buck populated with corn, sweet potatoes, regular white potatoes, tomatoes, cucumber, and a variety of other vegetables. We all got to participate in ensuring the garden flourished. Working in the garden was one of our summer chores.

Highlights

Mom canned the vegetables and made sure all the garden bounty was properly stored in the cool room. The crop of the cucumber that we didn't eat in a tomato and sliced cucumber salad, was put into large ceramic tubs, and turned into pickles.

She helped to keep milk cows, a sow with her piglets and a flock of chickens. The lucky chickens laid eggs. The much larger number of chickens were raised to be dinner. Most piglets got sold but a few made it into the freezer.

The cow milk was separated. Both the cream and the milk were sold. Some cream was churned into butter and some milk was made into yogurt.

During hunting season, she often went raccoon hunting with Buck and learned to cook raccoon and other wild game that he often brought back from hunting.

Mushroom hunting in late spring was an activity we all loved, and she would take us the spots in the woods most likely to have them.

The marriage hit bottom and Mom and Buck divorced. We moved to an apartment in Burlington.

At this point I started high school, and Mom had a second job as an Arthur Murray dance instructor.

Four years later, I was Senior in high school when Mom was diagnosed with tuberculosis, TB. In those days people with TB were sent to a TB sanitarium. The boys and I stayed in our apartment with several good friends helping us.

After my high school graduation, Conrad and I moved to Brazil. Ron stayed in Burlington to finishes his Senior year. He later ended up in the Navy.

At the sanitarium mom worked as a nurse's aide until the sanitarium closed.

Mom had inherited a plot of land in Brazil from her father. She hoped to use her inheritance, the deed to a property on a mountain side to improve the family fortune.

Her brother Conrad, Uncle Kutie, arranged for a trip home to Brazil on a German freighter, the Burg Sparenburg. It offered cabins for twelve passengers.

Highlights

On the way she met Uwe Sievert. He was the Chief Engineer on ship. They first met on the side deck as they left New York City. The two things she recalled was the beauty of the Verrazano bridge and the grandeur of the Statue of Liberty.

The inheritance in Brazil turned out to have been a swindle perpetrated on her father and she got no inheritance.

Her true inheritance was that she and Uwe dated and married. They were truly soul mates.

Soon after she decided to move us all back to the US.

Mom, Uwe, and Conrad found an Apartment in Freeport, Long Island.

Uwe remained on the Burg Sparenburg. Mom worked as surgical technician in a small hospital in Freeport. And Conrad went to school.

I returned to Urbana, Illinois and for a short period of time stayed with the Kitzmillers.

In 1969 Mom decided to move to Gulf Breeze, Florida that was just across the harbor from Pensacola. This location allowed Uwe more time at home from his continued work as a Chief Engineer on merchant ships.

She went to college and got her LPN license and worked in an office of an eye doctor.

She soon realized that she would do better selling insurance and went to work for New York Life insurance. She was back doing what she did very well in and enjoyed her work.

While living in the Florida panhandle Mom and Uwe enjoyed participating in the local German club, where made many friends and did a lot of dancing which they both enjoy greatly.

Later, after Conrad got married and left for the Airforce, they moved to Fort Walton and later built a lake side home on Lake Tantara.

Mom still sold insurance, but she also pursued her creative desire to paint. She took art classes in oil painting and even opened a craft shop and taught some art classes. She produced many paintings. The seaside and the ocean were her main focus.

Highlights

Uwe and Mom had an RV and were able to do some traveling.

However, in 1989, Uwe was diagnosed with ALS, he died in two years later. Mom sold the house on the lake and once again lived in Fort Walton in a condominium. After hurricane Hugo she sold the condominium and bought a large thirty-foot-long RV.

That is when Mom, Freddie and my daughter, Kimberly set off on their journey across the US. They visited various scenic locations, made friends along the way, and visited with family.

Mom eventually sold the RV and decided to move to Lakeland, Florida. Here she was close to the Kitzmiller's. This was about 1995. She bought a model home in a new housing development.

It had a nice back yard and as gardening was in her blood, her yard did thrive with flowers, trees, fruit trees, fruit vines and bushes. She also continued her love of painting. She sold many of her paintings or gave them to family and friends.

One the many things about Mom, was that she was always looking for a new project to do. She tried her hand at many things, making jewelry, painting cups, and traveling to new places.

Mom loved to entertain whether having family or friends. She was a terrific cook and was especially talented in fixing leftovers. She had many specialties dishes. Some were Brazilian, some were German, and of course many were American dishes.

One of Mom's other loves were her dogs and all animals. We had animals growing up. In Brazil, when we were young, we had a macaw that was blue and yellow. In in Urbana, growing up, we had dogs and a cat. In Iowa we had donkeys, Betsy, and her baby Smokey, we a cows that had to be milked, chickens, pigs, dogs, and cats.

In Florida Mom had Cleo a basset that she and Con got while in New York. Later in Fort Walton she got Freddie. He fathered a litter of puppies that were sold, but Conrad got one. The last dog she had at end of her time in Florida was a Westie named Bailey. She did a lot walking with Baily around the lake in her apartment complex.

Highlights

Mom spent the last five years or so living in an apartment in Lakeland and about a year or so in senior living home.

Alfredo, a retiree from New York, introduced to her by Rosemary Kitzmiller, became a close friend for many years. They did many things together. They traveled to visit family in New York, California, Ohio, and Illinois also in the Florida. Alfredo died about 6 months before I moved Mom to Illinois in 2014.

I brought her to Urbana, Illinois in 2014 where we set her up in an Alzheimer unit. Here she replaced Bailey with two baby dolls that the unit had, she rocked them, tried to feed them, and talked to them.

I visited frequently and we talked, sang children's songs in German and Brazilian and occasionally prayed.

Occasionally my two youngest grandchildren, Serra and Tyson went with me visit Mom. Mom would tell them about her babies. Occasionally she would dance with them and have a snack together and talk. One of the snacks that all of us enjoyed was guava and cheese.

Tyson's favorite past time was to tease her by pinching her nose or hiding her babies. He also would comb her hair or play with it. She really did enjoy their visits and I was grateful they were willing to go.

Mom died on June 9, 2017. She had chosen to be cremated. The family was able to meet in Pensacola in July 2018 to scatter her ashes in the Gulf of Mexico to join "the love of her life" Uwe.

I miss many of the things we did together like speaking Portuguese, or me trying to speak German, our sharing recollections of the past, and our phone calls. I miss the yearly visits to Florida. When the Joann and Kimberly were young, we spent many summer vacations by the beach and on the beach. Mom loved to take us site seeing in different parts of Florida.

She was a very brave lady of many talents and a driving desire to see her children do well.

She was a true trail blazer.

Dancing

By Joann, the oldest grand daughter

I was the first grand baby born to our amazing family. Oma and Opa were the most wonderful grandparents ever. They always made going to Florida the most amazing trip for us all, between great food, beach time, and great family stories.

When Oma would come to Illinois she would just freeze. I felt so bad, but it was so cute to see her in her coat and scarf in the house.

I would always learn so much from her and Opa about either family heritage or life in general. We have a very diverse family and I have always appreciated that. I am very proud of all our families' backgrounds. It makes us a very strong and unique family to have so much diversity.

I loved the drive to Florida every year. We would start out early in the morning and get there really late at night. I always knew when we were getting close, because you can smell the pine and the sea salt smell of the ocean.

Annelise Sievert

When we would get to Oma and Opa's they were usually still having their parties, or they were just finishing up. I was always allowed to sit at the breakfast bar or get a plate and sit on the couch and have a snack before bed. I felt like a big girl being able to have fun snacks and drinking out of a big girl cup; of course, I only got apple juice or something like that. One of my most favorite drinks to have was, Guarana Antarctica a Brazilian soft drink that has an apple flavor and a berry aftertaste. It has a lot of caffeine in it as well.

When I was 5 years old, I was lucky enough to have been able to visit Brazil to see my Great Oma. I was there with my parents, Oma, and Opa. It was such a great experience. There is a lot I don't remember, but there is a lot that I do. I remember the farm and the horses great Oma had on the farm. I got to see where my mom was born in Sao Paulo and where she grew up in Santos. I would love to go back now that I'm older and see it again. It was such an amazing experience as a kid. I feel so blessed to have been able to have gone. It was great to have been able to see my cousins in Brazil.

Cleo was Oma's Basset Hound, and she was so adorable. Her ears were so long so that when she would come running down the hallway, she would always step on them and trip and slide. It would always make me giggle.

Highlights

After Cleo Oma got Freddie. He was a Basset Hound as well. Oma chose to breed Freddie with another Basset Hound, and they had the cutest puppies with little freckles all over their body. Uncle Con and Aunt Susan got one of them and named it Freckles.

One memory that sticks with me still is the smell of Oma and her house. As a little girl I remember asking if I could use her smell good stuff in her bathroom that she used and she always said yes. Oma always let me take a little bottle with a black ball lid of Revlon Jean Nate Original After Bath Splash Mist to take home with me.

I remember getting up early to go out to the fig tree and try to beat the squirrels to the figs. We would pick whatever figs were ready to be picked, sometimes we would beat them and sometimes they would beat us. Oma's figs were so good! So, if we were lucky enough to beat the squirrels to the figs it was a great start to the morning.

Playing games after dinner was always so much fun every night or on a rainy day when we couldn't go to the beach. We would always play Yahtzee, and sometimes we would play Uno, go fish, Chinese checkers, and as we got older, we learned how to play Euchre.

We would look at family pictures and talk about everyone and how they were related to us.

Annelise Sievert

In Fort Walton Opa and I went hunting for clams. Walking around the pond and digging in the mud for clams you had to be quick before they went back into the mud. It was definitely something I had never done before, and it was such a great experience.

At the house by Lake Tentarra in De Funiak Springs I was able to do a lot of great things with Opa too. I got to help him in the yard doing different things with all the plants and garden. I learned so very much from him. He was a great man, strong, loving, caring, adoring husband, loving dad, and amazing Opa. When Opa got Lou Gehrig's Disease (ALS) I remember looking up as much information as I could on it at school. I did my own research, so I had a better understanding of the disease. Even though this disease was an ugly and painful one, Opa never complained from what I remember. He was such a strong old man.

The house really wasn't set up for Opa having this disease, however Oma was so amazing to him and had his bed put in the living room so he could look out of the porch sliding glass doors to the lake. He could see the sunrise, watch his hummingbirds dance around, and see all his beautiful plants. Freddie would sleep with him in his bed and Oma would sleep on the couch next to him. I remember being told that Freddie woke up Oma after Opa passed.

One year, when I was in my early teens, I went down to Florida two weeks before mom and dad.

Oma, Opa, and I did all kinds of things together.

Highlights

One of the things on my list that I thought would be fun to do is to pick my own crab to eat. So, we went down to the docks, and I was able to pick my own blue crab. They were still in water and still moving around when I picked them out, so they were very fresh. They had just come off the boat. However, what we found out later is they had been in the sun too long because I got horribly sick.

Once I started feeling better, we went to the beach every day, which was amazing.

Oma asked me what I was doing in school and what I was interested in besides my sports. I told Oma I was interested in drawing and painting.

So, Oma and I worked on some really neat paintings. It was fun to draw with Oma and paint with her. I didn't realize the talent Oma had nor did she realize the talent her granddaughter had until we painted and drew together.

It felt so good to impress Oma and Opa both.

Nick loved Oma. He wasn't around her a lot, but whenever she came to Illinois, she was always so excited to see him. He was always excited to be able to go over to grandma and grandpa Hart's house to see everyone and then see Oma too.

Serra loves her Oma very much. I truly wish she could have had the time I had with Oma. However, the time she did get, she remembers sitting with Oma in the kids' room at mom and dad's house while Oma was visiting us in Illinois.

They would look through Oma's jewelry and talk about where some pieces came from or what pieces meant to her. Oma gave her a bracelet one time that meant the world to Serra. Serra was never able to go to Florida to see Oma, so it was so extra special to get a bracelet from Oma and all the stories that came with it.

In the years that followed, as Oma's health started to fail and she had to come to Illinois, Serra and I would go see Oma at the facility where she was staying.

She was the light of the place which should not surprise anyone. She had the health care workers on their toes and in stitches. They all loved her to pieces and so did most of the other residents. They would do so many fun game nights, cooking, and do one of Oma's most favorite things, DANCING! She would get everyone to dance, the workers, husbands with their wives, and people who didn't think they could. She just always loved to have a great time.

One memory Serra has the most, is that there were these two baby dolls in the hallway that Oma asked if she could have. She took very good care of these two baby dolls. I think near the end she needed that and that is how I explained it to Serra. Serra got to go on some walks with Oma and with me which I am so very thankful for.

At the very end Mom, Kimmie and I sat with Oma and held her hand to let her know it would be ok. Opa would be waiting for her so they could dance again.

Love you so very much Omie.

Highlights

Always in my thoughts and Heart
By Conrad, the young and handsome one.

I am the youngest of three children. My wife and daughters tell me I am also the good looking one.

I was 10 going on 11 when our Mother was diagnosed with tuberculosis. She went to a tuberculosis center to live where she received her treatments.

My sister and I were sent to live with our Uncle Conrad's family in Santos, Brazil.

From my perspective it was a difficult time trying to keep up with the fast paced changes that were occurring in my life. My sister is 8 years older and I'm sure she was as traumatized as I was but with a much better understanding of what was happening.

I was heartbroken leaving my Mother and I would not see her again until almost a year and a half later.

In those days talking on an oversees call required the help of the operator who would call you back once a connection was made with the intended party. Consequently, I only remember talking to my mother once at Christmas time during the time we were apart.

We did write letters to each other and receiving a letter from my mother was always the best feeling in the world.

We went back to the US in 1967 and again my life became a whirlwind of change.

My mother was newly wed to Hans Uwe Sievert.

My brother, Ron was in the Navy

And my sister moved back to and started her new life in Champagne, Illinois

This time instead of trying to keep up with my brother, I was trying to keep up with my mother.

She and I moved to Long Island, NY by ourselves. Uwe remained on as the Chief Engineer on the Burg Sparenburg.

We went Apartment hunting and found a place in Freeport NY.

We adopted a Bassett hound named Cleo.

Mom found a job as a surgical nurse at the local hospital. She would come home from a long day of surgeries and tell me about during surgery holding someone's heart in her hands and how she was so amazed by that. I often thought this was her most difficult job of the many she had. She was on her feet all day dealing with not only the physical challenges but also the emotional ones.

The highs were good, but the lows included the deaths of patients.

Highlights

Of course, mom was never one to stay in one place too long and Long Island was no exception. After a couple of years, I was told we were moving to Florida where Uwe would have more time at home from his Merchant Marine job.

In typical fashion my mother rented a U-Haul. She had no worries about driving a truck. We loaded all our possessions and headed to Pensacola, Florida.

I was too young to drive so we had a fun road trip with Mom driving a truck and our Basset Hound between us.

I had no idea where we would be living but she had that all planned out and quickly I learned to love my new home.

It turns out I would meet my wife there. As of this writing we have been together for 46 years.

I like to think I became as adventurous or brave as my mother was but in no way have I approached her level of life changing decisions.

I know she instilled a work ethic in her children that still serves us today.

I miss her but often look back at those moments with love and laughter.

She is always with me in thought and in my heart.

Annelise Sievert

Highlights

Epilogue
By Ron

The years have passed, and my mother is now the angel that she played in her young age.

Her last marriage was to Hans Uwe Sievert the Chief Engineer she met on one of her trips to Brazil. I wish she had met him earlier in her life and that he could have been my father. His story has many twists, and he lived a good life. At end he suffered from Lou Gehrig's disease.

My mother never remarried but had a companion, Alfredo, for many years.

Marlene, her oldest daughter is now seventy-six years old. She has been married for 52 years to Richard Hart. They have two daughters and 2 grandchildren.

She lives in Urbana, Illinois that is just a few miles from Rantoul where my mother first lived when we got to the US.

As a young girl, she and my younger brother returned with our mother to Brazil. They lived there for less than two years.

It turned out that the land granted to our mother by her father was never legally his. The person selling it to him had falsified the records. My mother inherited nothing.

Conrad, her brother inherited a very successful engineering construction business.

Marlene returned to Urbana on her return to the US and met Richard.

My six-year younger brother, Conrad a veteran of the Airforce and a successful businessman has been married to Susan, his high school sweetheart for forty six years. has three daughters, Bridget, Rachel, and Ashley that were always my mother's sweethearts.

They are all married and have children.

Conrad is grandfather to eight children.

His wife of forty six years, Susan still thinks he is the best looking and most loving man she ever met.

It seems odd for me to think of my, "little brother" as a grandfather.

I guess I am the oldest even though I am in the middle. I have had a grand life. Left Burlington High School in 1968 and entered the Navy.

In the Navy, I became an Electronics Technician (ET) and expected to go to Nuclear Power operator school immediately after becoming an ET. However, I had to wait for the Nuclear Power school start date.

During my wait I was put on board the USS Gunstan Hall and ended up in Vietnam. There I volunteered to be on a fifty-caliber machine gun and to escort the Tango Boats that went upriver to open them up.

After that tour, I did ended up in the Nuclear Operator training program.

However, I never became a nuclear reactor operator.

I volunteered for a tour of duty on the hydrofoil Tucumcari. On it I toured all the coastal countries of Europe.

Upon return I was reassigned to decommission a ship. During that time, I facilitated the end of the ship's race riot and received and early out as a reward.

I then attended Pensacola Junior College and the University of South Florida and graduated with a master's degree in mechanical engineering.

Highlights

I was fortunate to meet Hien, now my wife of fifty years at Pensacola Junior College. We have three children, Thu, Kurt, and Derek. They all successfully graduated from college.

There are three grand Children, Courtney, Christine, and David Huynh

I went to work for Procter and Gamble and thirty-eight years later I retired.

I then pursued my dream, and the dream that my mother had of writing.

I have more than twenty books and continue to write.

Putting together and editing highlights is my tribute to my mother.

She was my inspiration.
        She was the warm upward wind that carried me up
                from the lows and
                    let me soar.

Annelise Sievert

Highlights

More About Annelise Sievert

Her Writer's Bio.

Born in Brazil to German immigrants, Annelise was the blonde, blue eyed, pixie tom boy. Her young life was spent climbing eucalyptus trees, running through the woods, and telling adventure stories to her younger brother and his friends. She became a nurse but then soon a housewife and a mother of three. When her marriage came apart, she left Brazil with her three children.

She was sponsored by an American family, the Kitzmiller's, who had been her back door neighbors in Sao Paulo. Rosemary Kitzmiller, the oldest daughter, became a lifelong friend to Annelise.

Never one to stand still, she tried many ways to make an income. She was a clerk at an Air Force PX but soon realized she was making much less than her male counter parts. She decided to try Insurance Sales. This was a field that allowed her competitive spirit to flourish, and she became a star performer. Along the way she also taught at Arthur Murray dance studios, worked in a variety of clerking and sales roles. She was always trying to get ahead.

She pushed her kids to do well and to seek success.

Her father left her the deed to a large track of land in Brazil. Soon after her father's death Annelise decided to return and see if she could make something out of her inheritance. The dream of success and wealth quickly turned to disappointment when she discovered the deed to the land was a fake. Her father had been swindled and she was left with nothing; nothing but her own internal strength.

Annelise Sievert

On her way back to Brazil she met Uwe Sievert. He turned out to be the persons she had sought all her life. He was truly her soul mate. She married and returned to the United States. Florida became her home and life with Uwe was good.

Along the way she became a painter and she taught painting as well.

She also dabbled at writing. She wrote pieces of many stories but never quite finished them.

Highlights

About the Son

Ronald E. Mueller

remwriter95@gmail.com

Ron grew up in what is now Flint River State Park in Southeast Iowa. The 170-year-old house Ron lived in is built into a hillside. It faces a 125-foot-high cliff towering over the little Flint River. The house and the land talked to him about; the passing of time, the struggle to conquer the land, the struggles people faced and the wonder of nature.

He climbed the cliffs, crawled into the caves, dove from the swimming rock, collected clams from the bottom of the pond, gigged and skinned frogs for their legs. He trapped muskrats for fur, hunted raccoon in the dead of night, and with only a stick hunted rabbits in the dead of winter.

His young life was outdoors, and nature tested him.

He walked to a one room stone schoolhouse uphill both ways. A stern but warm-hearted teacher, Mrs. Henry was instrumental in shaping his character as she shepherded him from the fourth to the eighth grade. A Montessori before its time. It was a great way to grow up.

His experiences inter-twined with snippets of fantasy lend themselves to the adventures he leads the reader through.

He in his now old age has edited and published Highlights and has fulfilled his mother's dream that he adopted. He has become a writer.

His books:

The Alex Evercrest Series:
    The River Front
    The Girl on the Grill
    Missing
    Maggot
    Racist
    Votive Candles

The Taelo Series:
    Taelo: The Early Years
    Taelo: The Golden Feather
    Taelo: Journey of Discovery
    Taelo: Dangerous Passage
    Taelo: Condor Clan Slingers
    Taelo: Circumvention

A Taelo Story:
    The Name of the Child
    White Swan and Quiet Pheasant
    Broken Spear
    Floating Cloud
    Quiet Rabbit
    Busy Bee
    Little Otter& Talking Wren
    Burley Bear & Meadow Flower

A Feather-in-the-Wind Story:
    The Eastern Elk Clan

Science Fiction Books by Ron Mueller
    The Door Series:
        The Door
        Delivery
        Journey Beyond
    The Savitar Series:
        Journey's End

Highlights

Savitar
Confluence
Single Science Fiction Books:
    Current Past and Future
    Event Survivors
Fiction Books by Ron Mueller
    The Problem Solver
Imagination by Courtney Huynh and Chloe Parker

Annelise Sievert

Published by: Around the World Publishing LLC.

QR Links to
ATWP.US web site

www.ingramcontent.com/pod-product-compliance
Lightning Source LLC
Chambersburg PA
CBHW071912070526
44583CB00016B/1960